SCIENCE ANSWERS

Solids, Liquids, and Gases

FROM ICE CUBES TO BUBBLES

Heinemann Library
Chicago, Illinois

Carol Ballard

Design: Jo Hinton-Malivoire and
  Tinstar Design Ltd (www.tinstar.co.uk)
Illustrations: Jeff Edwards
Picture Research: Rosie Garai
  and Liz Eddison
Originated by Dot Gradations Ltd.
Printed in China by WKT Co.Ltd
08 07 06
10 9 8 7 6 5

Library of Congress Cataloging-in-Publication Data

Ballard, Carol.
  Solids, liquids, and gases : from ice cubes
to bubbles / Carol Ballard.
      v. cm. -- (Science answers)
Includes bibliographical references and
index.
Contents: What are solids, liquids and
gases? -- What are solids, liquids and gases
made from? -- How do solids, liquids and
gases move and change? -- Can solids
become liquids? -- Can liquids become
gases?-- What is the water cycle? -- Can all
changes go backwards and forwards? --
What is a solution?
  ISBN 1-4034-0955-2 (HC), 1-4034-3552-9
(pbk.)
  1. Matter--Properties--Juvenile literature.
[1. Matter--Properties.]
I. Title. II. Series.
  QC173.36.B35 2003
  530.4--dc21
                    2003003763

Acknowledgments
The author and publishers are grateful to
the following for permission to reproduce
copyright material:

pp. 4, 5, 27 Liz Eddison; p. 6 Photodisc;
pp. 8, 11, 17, 22, 26 Trevor Clifford; p. 12
Packert White/Getty Images; p. 13 Annie
Griffiths Belt/Corbis/; p. 14 Science Photo
Library/Phil Jude; p. 15, 28 (bottom), 28
(top) Science Photo Library; p. 16 Charles
D. Winters/Science Photo Library; p. 21
Tom Stewart/Corbis; p. 21 Donna
Day/Corbis; p. 24 Taxi/Tudor Photography;
p. 28 (middle) Sheila Terry/Science Photo
Library.

Cover photograph of the Pahoehoe
lava flow, Kilauea Volcano, Hawaii
reproduced with permission of Getty
Images/G. Brad Lewis.

Some words are shown in
bold, **like this.** You can find
out what they mean by
looking in the glossary

Contents

About the experiments and demonstrations

In each chapter of this book you will find a section called Science Answers. It describes an experiment or demonstration that you can try yourself. There are some simple safety rules to follow when doing an experiment:
• Ask an adult to help with any cutting using a sharp knife.
• Electrical sockets are dangerous. Never, ever try to experiment with them.
• Do not use any experimental **materials** near an electrical socket.

Materials you will use

Most of the experiments and demonstrations in this book can be done with objects you can find in your own home. A few will need items you can buy from a hardware store. You will also need paper and a pencil to record your results.

What Are Solids, Liquids, and Gases?

The **states of matter** are solid, liquid, and gas. There are solids, liquids, and gases all around you. Wood, metal, plastic, and stone are solids. Water, ink, blood, and orange juice are liquids. The air is a **mixture** of different gases. Solids, liquids, and gases move and change in different ways and have different uses.

Using solids

Solid **materials** are used to make many different things. Some solids, such as stone, are hard and strong and are good for building. Other solids, such as feathers, are soft and are perfect for filling pillows and cushions. Some solids are stretchy, like elastic, but others, like wood, do not stretch at all. Some, like metal, can be sharpened. Some, like plastics, can be molded into different shapes and dyed bright colors. All these materials are very different, but they are all solids.

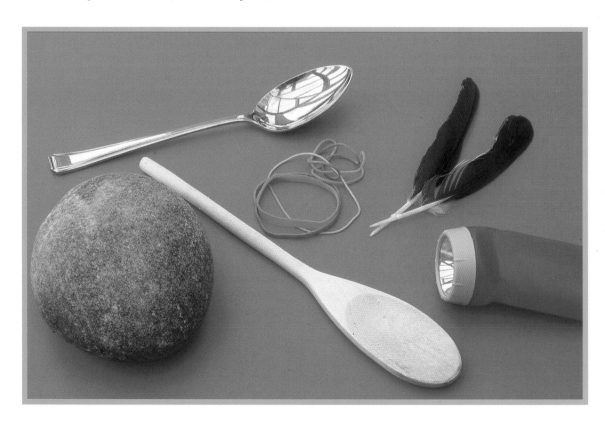

Life-giving water

The most important liquid is water. You need to drink a lot of water to keep your body healthy. You use water for many other things, too—cooking, washing yourself and the things you use, swimming and playing in swimming pools, and sailing and surfing on lakes and the sea. Water that sprays into the air from fountains makes parks and gardens look attractive. Farmers and gardeners spray water on crops and other plants to help them grow.

Using other liquids

Many other things around you are liquids, too. Ketchup, hot chocolate, and orange juice are tasty liquids to eat and drink. Cooking oil is used for frying foods such as potato chips. Your pen would not write without ink, and car engines need gasoline. Oil keeps **machines** working smoothly, and dishwashing liquid helps clean dirty dishes. Many things that you use to keep yourself clean are liquids, such as shampoo and some soaps.

Using gases

Most gases are invisible, but that does not mean they are not important. When you breathe in, you take in a gas called oxygen from the air to stay alive. You get rid of waste carbon dioxide when you breathe out. Carbon dioxide is put into some drinks to make them fizzy. Air is pumped into the tires of cars and bicycles to help cushion bumpy rides. Helium is a gas that is lighter than air, so a balloon filled with helium will float away unless you hold it down. Many houses have gas fireplaces and gas stoves that burn natural gas. They give out heat that can be used for heating or cooking. Camp stoves and gas grills use other gases, such as propane, as fuel.

Air

The atmosphere that surrounds the earth is a layer of air about 310 miles (500 kilometers) thick. Without the atmosphere, nothing could live on the earth. The air is a **mixture** of different gases. Nitrogen makes up just under four-fifths of the air, one-fifth is oxygen, and there are tiny amounts of other gases, such as carbon dioxide and argon.

What Are Solids, Liquids, and Gases Made From?

Everything around you is made of very tiny pieces of matter. The tiniest pieces of anything are called **atoms.** These are joined together to make bigger pieces called **molecules.** It is hard to imagine, but molecules are so tiny that there are millions and millions in a single grain of sand. Each **material** is made up of its own special molecules. The molecules in solids, liquids, and gases are arranged in different ways.

Patterns of molecules

In a solid, the molecules are lined up in a tight, regular pattern. They are very close together, and each one is held in place by the other molecules around it. They cannot move around at all.

The molecules are freer in a liquid than in a solid. They are spaced out and arranged in a loose pattern. They are not held together tightly, so they can move about and change places with other molecules close to them.

Molecules of gases are not held together at all. They move about **randomly** all the time and are not arranged in a pattern.

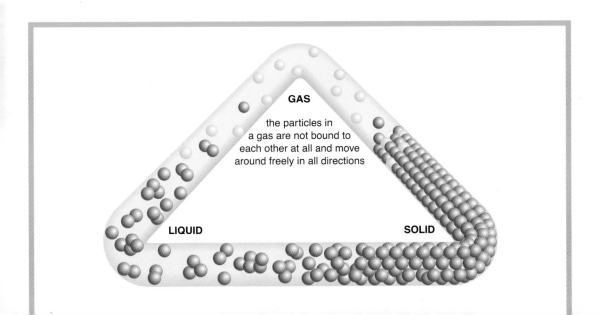

GAS

the particles in a gas are not bound to each other at all and move around freely in all directions

LIQUID

SOLID

EXPERIMENT: Why does water change color when liquid dye is added?

HYPOTHESIS

The molecules of the dye are able to move through the water and spread out. This movement results in color being seen throughout the water.

EQUIPMENT

A clear plastic container, cold water, colored food dye (washable if possible), a pipette or eyedropper

EXPERIMENT STEPS

1. Half-fill your container with cold water.
2. Place it carefully on a table and wait until the water looks absolutely still.
3. Suck up a few drops of dye with your pipette or eyedropper.
4. Carefully squeeze one or two drops into the water.
5. Watch what happens.
6. Write down what you saw.

CONCLUSION

There are spaces between the molecules in a liquid and they are able to move around. Because you mixed two liquids, their molecules mixed together freely, and the color spread throughout the water.

How Do Solids, Liquids, and Gases Move and Change?

Solids, liquids, and gases all move and change in different ways. There are three questions you can ask about something to find out whether it is a solid, a liquid, or a gas.

1. Does it change its shape?

Solids only change their shape if a **force** is applied to them. A lump of clay keeps its shape until you pull, push, squeeze, and stretch it into a new shape. But liquids and gases do not keep their shape. If you pour orange juice out of a carton into a glass, it spreads out to take the exact shape of the glass. When you blow up a balloon, the air you breathe out spreads out to completely fill the shape of the balloon.

2. Does it flow?

Solids cannot flow because their **molecules** are held together too tightly. But liquids and gases can flow easily. You can pour a liquid from one container into another container—for example, when you turn on a tap, water flows out of the pipe and into your glass. Liquids spread out on their own, too. If you spill some paint, it does not just stay in a lump but flows and spreads out to cover a bigger space. Gases also flow freely, as you can feel when you untie the knot on a balloon and the air inside flows out.

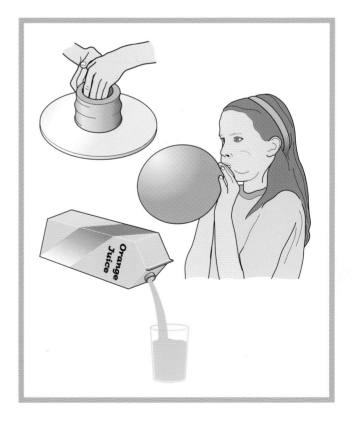

3. Does it always take up the same amount of space?

The amount of space something takes up is called its **volume.** A solid brick does not change its shape, so it will always have the same volume.

If you pour a quart (liter) of milk out of a carton into a measuring cup, it will be a different shape but there will still be exactly one quart (liter) of milk. So liquids change their shape but always have the same volume.

When air freshener is sprayed out of a can at one side of a room, it slowly spreads across the room until eventually people at the other side are able to smell it. This is because gases do not always have the same volume. They spread out to fill all the space they possibly can.

By asking these three questions, you can decide whether something is a solid, a liquid, or a gas.

This table shows the answers:

question	solids	liquids	gases
Does it change its shape?	no	yes	yes
Does it flow?	no	yes	yes
Does it always have the same volume?	yes	yes	no

DEMONSTRATION: The temperature of a liquid can affect how fast it will flow.

EQUIPMENT
A 12-inch (30-centimeter) ruler, honey, something to lean the ruler on (such as a large book in a plastic bag or a pencil case), an eyedropper, a stopwatch or wristwatch with a second hand, a small drinking glass, a tablespoon, a small bowl of hot water

DEMONSTRATION STEPS
1. With the ruler flat on the table, put some honey on it to fill the space between the 1 and 2.
2. Carefully lean the ruler against the book with the 0 at the top and start the clock.
3. Write down how far the honey traveled in 10 seconds.
4. Wash your ruler.
5. Put two tablespoons of honey in the drinking glass. Stand the glass in the bowl of hot water. You may have to steady it to keep it from tipping. Let the honey warm up for about 3 or 4 minutes.
6. Repeat steps 1, 2, and 3 with the warm honey.
7. Write down what you saw.

EXPLANATION
Warming a liquid will make it flow faster, because the **molecules** move around faster and through greater distances within the liquid.

Can Solids Become Liquids?

You can keep things cold in a freezer. When you take something out of the freezer, it is hard and solid. When you take ice cubes out of the freezer and put them in a warmer place, the solid ice slowly turns into liquid. When this happens, the ice is said to **melt.** Ice and liquid water are made up of exactly the same **molecules.** The only difference is that the molecules are arranged in a different way. This is a **physical change** and is called a **change of state.**

Melting popsicles

If you don't eat your popsicle quickly enough on a hot day, it will melt and drip all over the place! The heat from the air around you melts the frozen juice, changing it from a solid into a liquid.

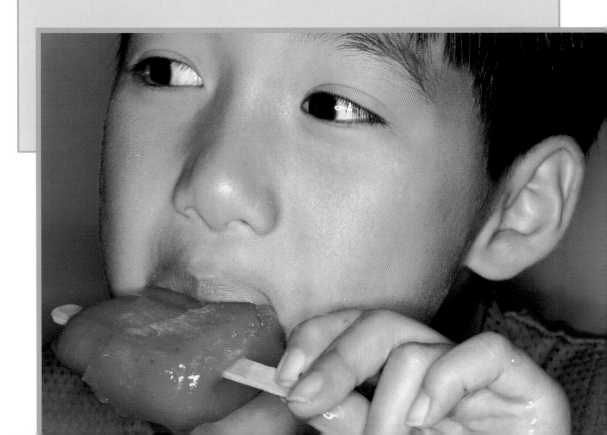

Back and forth

Changing states from a solid to a liquid is a **reversible** change. This means that it can go backward or forward. You can change a solid into a liquid and then change the liquid back into a solid again!

Getting colder

When you cool a liquid, it gets colder and colder until at last it changes into a solid. This change is called **freezing.** Water freezes at 32 °F (0 °C). This temperature is its freezing point. If you put liquid water into an ice-cube tray and put it into the freezer, it will turn into solid ice.

Other liquids change into solids as they cool, too. Different liquids become solids at different temperatures. Liquid wax from a candle may drip down, but as it cools it will turn back into solid wax. Liquid rock pours out of a volcano but changes into solid rock as it cools.

Freezing cold!

If it is cold where you live, you can see things freezing all around you in winter. Puddles freeze and water drips to form icicles. When the air is cold, rain freezes and falls as snow or hail.

Can Liquids Become Gases?

If you place a bowl of water on a table, there will be less water in the bowl after several days. Where does the water go? It **evaporates** into a gas. The liquid and the gas are made up of exactly the same **molecules.** The only difference is that the molecules are arranged in a different way. This is another **change of state.** The gas molecules have moved into the air around them.

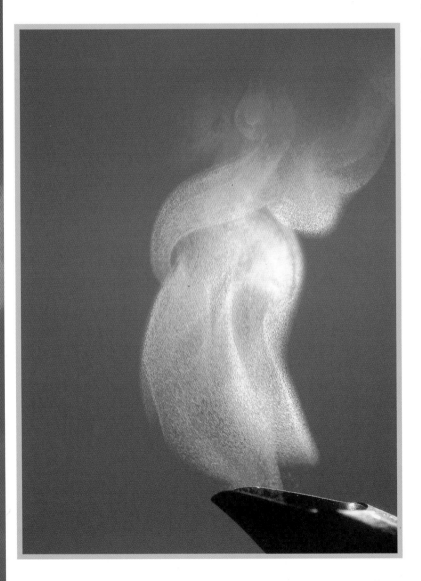

You can heat liquids, too. They get hotter and hotter until at last they cannot stay liquid any more. When this happens, it is said that the liquid turns into a **vapor.** The more quickly a liquid is heated, the more quickly it becomes a vapor.

Boiling water

When you heat water on the stove, it gets hotter and hotter. When the temperature of the water reaches 212 °F (100 °C), the water boils. The water cannot remain a liquid when it is this hot. It turns into a gas called steam or water vapor. Different liquids have different boiling points at which they turn into a vapor.

Changing a liquid into a gas is a **reversible** change. If you cool a gas, it will turn back into a liquid.

If you breathe out hard on a cold day, you can see a stream of white blowing into the air. The warm air from inside your body cools quickly when it mixes with the cold air outside. Water vapor in your breath turns back into liquid water, and you see the tiny droplets of liquid water. When a gas changes back into a liquid it is said to be **condensing.**

All steamed up!

When a gas cools, it turns back into a liquid. Water evaporates from a hot bath and becomes water vapor. When the water vapor hits a cold surface such as a glass window or mirror, it cools down very quickly. It turns back into liquid water that you see as a misty layer.

Some **materials** can change their state only if they are very hot or very cold.

Most metals need to be heated to a very high temperature before they will **melt** and turn into liquids. Gold has to be heated to more than 1,832 °F (1,000 °C) for it to melt, and iron does not melt until it is hotter than 2,732 °F (1,500 °C). That is really hot—nearly eight times hotter than an oven needs to be to cook a pizza!

Most gases need to be extremely cold before they will change into liquids. Both oxygen and nitrogen change from gas to liquid at nearly -328 °F (-200 °C). That is about ten times colder than an ordinary freezer!

An unusual gas

Carbon dioxide is an unusual gas. It changes from a solid to a gas without being a liquid in between. Solid carbon dioxide is sometimes used in theaters. As the solid warms up, white clouds of gas slowly move across the stage, creating eerie, misty effects.

EXPERIMENT: If a solid is changed to a liquid, will it weigh the same?

HYPOTHESIS
Warming a substance will change its **state of matter,** but it will not change its weight.

EQUIPMENT
A few ice cubes, three plastic beakers, tape, a marker, a thermometer, a scale

EXPERIMENT STEPS
1. Put the ice cubes in the three beakers. Label the beakers 1, 2, and 3. Push the thermometer down into one beaker. Measure and record the temperature, then remove the thermometer.
2. Weigh each beaker with its ice cubes. Record the weights.
3. Put the beakers in a warm place, perhaps on a windowsill.
4. Remove beaker 1 after 10 minutes, beaker 2 after 20 minutes, and beaker 3 after 30 minutes. Upon removing each beaker, measure the temperature of the melted ice cubes and then weigh the beaker.
5. Write down the temperature and weight for each beaker.

CONCLUSION
As the temperature increased, the ice changed from solid to liquid. The weight of the ice and the water after the ice melted were the same. No matter was lost or gained when the ice changed from solid to liquid.

ADDITIONAL EXPERIMENTS
Try starting with more or fewer ice cubes or using a different type of container— do they make any difference?

What Is the Water Cycle?

Water is very important to every living thing. Without water, nothing could live. Water covers 71 percent of the earth. Some, such as water in the oceans and seas, is salty. Some, such as water in lakes and rivers, is not salty. All around you, every minute of every day, water is moving and changing from solid to liquid to gas and back again. These changes, which go around and around and never stop, are called the water cycle.

You can start with the sea

When the sun shines on the sea water, it warms it up. Some water gets so warm that it **evaporates.** It turns from liquid water into water **vapor.** This warm water vapor rises higher and higher into the sky.

The higher the water vapor rises, the colder the air around it gets. This cools the water vapor. At last, the water vapor gets so cold that it turns back into liquid water. The droplets of liquid water form clouds.

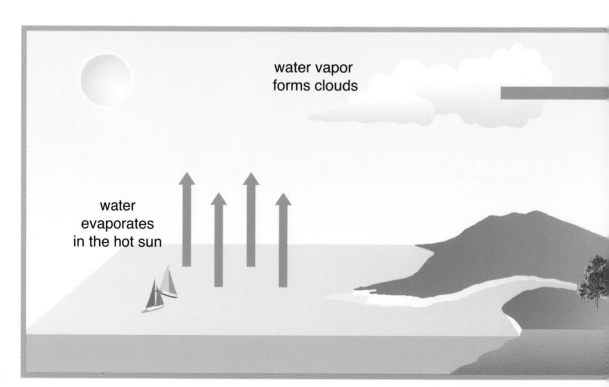

water vapor
forms clouds

water
evaporates
in the hot sun

Clouds are blown across the sky by the wind. Water droplets in the clouds group together to make bigger droplets. When they get too big, they fall down to the earth as rain. As the clouds rise higher in the sky, they get colder and colder. If the clouds get really cold, the water droplets may turn into ice **crystals.** These fall to the earth as snow or hail. Water falling to the earth as rain, snow, or hail is called **precipitation.** Most of the rain seeps through the land into streams or rivers, that flow to the sea. Then the cycle begins again.

Rain, streams, and rivers

Some rain soaks into the rocks and reappears as a spring further on. Some rain trickles over the surface of the ground, making tiny streams. These join together to make rivers. All the rivers flow back to the sea—and the whole cycle begins again.

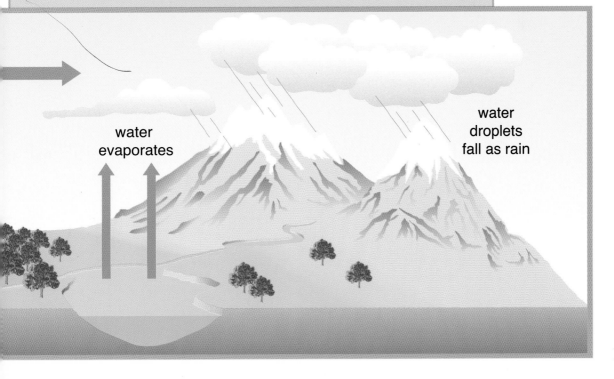

water
evaporates

water
droplets
fall as rain

EXPERIMENT: How do clouds form?

HYPOTHESIS
Clouds form when water **vapor** cools.

EQUIPMENT
A few ice cubes, plastic wrap, a tall glass jar with a metal lid (such as a jelly jar or pickle jar), hot (not boiling) water

EXPERIMENT STEPS
1. Wrap some ice cubes in plastic wrap.
2. Half-fill your jar with hot water. (It is a good idea to get an adult to help you.)
3. Put the lid on the jar.
4. Put your wrapped ice cubes on top of the lid.
5. Watch what happens inside the jar just under the lid.
6. Write down what you saw.

CONCLUSION
When water vapor cools down, it **condenses** into water droplets. This is how clouds form. The ice cubes cool the water vapor in the jar in exactly the same way that the cold air in the atmosphere cools the warm water vapor that rises from the sea.

Can All Changes Go Backward and Forward?

Physical changes of state are **reversible.** This means they can go backward and forward. For example, you can change water into ice and ice back into water. Not all changes can do this. Some can only go one way and can never go backward. These **irreversible** changes are **chemical changes.**

Burning is a chemical change that can only go one way. When you burn wood, the bright flames provide light and warmth. Smoke spirals up into the air. When the fire goes out, you are left with just a pile of ashes. This is all that is left of the wood. It has been changed forever. You cannot get back the wood that you started with.

Clay and pottery

Potters use clay to make their pots and jugs. While the clay is soft and wet, they can make it into all kinds of shapes. Then they put it into a very hot oven called a kiln. When the clay comes out of the kiln, it is dry and hard. The potter cannot get the soft, wet clay back. It has changed forever.

Irreversible changes happen when you cook things. If you fry an egg, you can never change it back into a raw egg, can you? And once bread has been toasted, it can never be changed back into ordinary bread again.

Plaster models

You can make models using a fine white powder called **plaster of Paris.** When this is mixed with water, it makes a runny white liquid. If you pour it into a **mold** and leave it for a while, it slowly becomes hard and solid. The water **molecules** become locked to the plaster molecules and cannot be separated. When you take it out of the mold, it keeps the shape of the mold it was in. You can paint and decorate your model, but you cannot get the white powder back again. This is an irreversible, **chemical change.**

Burning, cooking, and making pottery and plaster models are just some of the ways you use **chemical changes.** You do many other things that involve chemical changes, too.

A complete change

Some chemical changes make new **materials.** For example, heating sand and limestone together makes glass. When the sand and limestone get very hot, a chemical change happens and they turn into glass. Some special types of glue come in two separate tubes. When you mix the substances from the two tubes together, a chemical change occurs. The new material makes a very, very strong bond.

Dyes are special chemicals used to change the color of things. When you mix fabric with dye, a chemical change binds them together so that the dye changes the color of the fabric. **Bleach** does the opposite. It change dyes so that the colors fade or disappear completely, leaving a faded or white fabric.

Photographs

When you take a photograph using an ordinary camera, a chemical change happens as light hits the photographic film. More chemical changes are needed to finally develop and print pictures from the film.

DEMONSTRATION: Baking soda is a solid in the form of a powder. Lemon juice is a liquid. If you combine them, a chemical change will take place.

EQUIPMENT

A clear plastic tube or bottle with a small neck, lemon juice, sodium bicarbonate (baking soda), a balloon

DEMONSTRATION STEPS

(Hint: This can get messy, so it's a good idea to do it over a sink or large bowl.)

1. Pour some lemon juice into your bottle.
2. Add a teaspoon of sodium bicarbonate.
3. Quickly fit the balloon over the neck of the bottle.
4. Watch what happens.
5. The fizziness shows that a chemical reaction is taking place.
6. Write down what you saw.

EXPLANATION

When you add sodium bicarbonate to lemon juice, you can see that a **chemical change** takes place. The liquid and the powder make a gas. The gas rises up out of the bottle and fills the balloon.

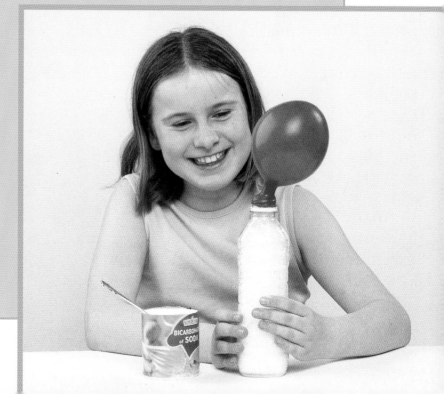

24

What Is a Solution?

If you stir a teaspoon of sugar into a cup of water, the sugar will slowly disappear. The water stays clear and the sugar vanishes. If you taste the water, however, it will be sweet. So the sugar must still be there, even if you cannot see it. When you add sugar to water, you create a **mixture.** When sugar mixes with water this way, the solid has **dissolved.** The sugary water is called a sugar **solution.**

In some mixtures, such as rice and sand, you can always see both substances clearly. So, all solutions are mixtures, but not all mixtures are solutions.

How temperature affects solutions

Many people add sugar to hot drinks such as tea or coffee. The hotter the liquid, the faster the **molecules** move around. This makes the spaces between them bigger, so the sugar molecules can find a space more quickly. It takes longer to dissolve sugar in cold water than in hot water.

The form that sugar is in affects how quickly it dissolves. Sugar grains dissolve more quickly than lumps or cubes. This is because the separate grains can spread through the water more quickly than bigger lumps. Sugar is not the only solid that dissolves in water. Other solids can dissolve, too. For example, the sea is a solution of water with salt dissolved in it. Some solids will not dissolve in water but will dissolve in a different liquid such as alcohol or oil.

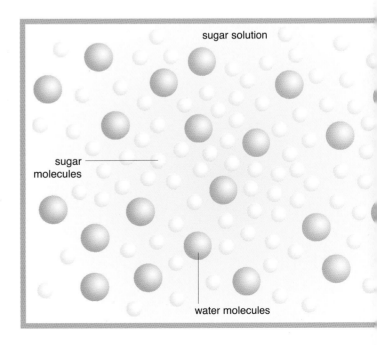

sugar solution

sugar molecules

water molecules

Solution or suspension?

Sometimes a solid does not **dissolve** in liquid, but it does not settle to the bottom, either. It also does not float on top of the liquid. The **molecules** of the solid float throughout the liquid and give it a cloudy **appearance.** This is called a **suspension.** If a suspension is left undisturbed for a while, the solid will eventually sink to the bottom.

Stirring things up

Stirring liquids speeds up dissolving, too. It spreads the molecules of the solid throughout the liquid so they can find the spaces more quickly.

DEMONSTRATION: Make your own solutions, mixtures, and suspensions

EQUIPMENT
Five disposable plastic containers; water; one teaspoon each of: sugar, sand, salt, flour, **plaster of Paris;** five disposable plastic spoons

DEMONSTRATION STEPS
1. Half-fill each container with water.
2. Put one teaspoon of sugar into the first container and stir. Repeat, putting sand into the second container, salt into the third, flour into the fourth, and plaster of Paris into the fifth.
3. Allow the containers to stand for about 30 minutes.
4. Write down what you see happening in each container.

EXPLANATION
Some solids dissolve in water, but others do not. Sand molecules are much larger and heavier than those of water, so the sand sinks to the bottom. Sugar water and salt water are **solutions;** sand and water form a **mixture;** flour and plaster of Paris each form suspensions when mixed with water.

People Who Found the Answers

John Dalton (1766-1844)

John Dalton was an English scientist. One of his most important ideas was his atomic theory, which said that everything is made up of tiny pieces called **atoms.** He tried to use this idea to explain how solids and liquids move and change, and how **chemical changes** happen.

Joseph Priestley (1733-1804)

Joseph Priestley was an English church minister who also did a lot of experiments. He discovered nitrogen and oxygen (although a Swedish scientist named Scheele said he had actually discovered oxygen first). Joseph also invented the first fizzy soft drink!

Antoine Lavoisier (1743-1794)

Antoine Lavoisier lived and worked in France. He was a scientist and politician. One of his most important discoveries was how oxygen is important in burning and breathing. He also developed one of the first systems for naming chemicals.

Amazing Facts

- You might find it hard to believe, but glass is really a liquid! You cannot see it flowing, because it is very, very thick and flows extremely slowly. Over hundreds of years, it will slowly flow downward—so very old glass windows are thicker at the bottom than at the top!

- Water does not always boil at exactly 212 °F (100 °C). At sea level, this is the boiling point of water, but as you climb higher, the boiling point gets lower. At the top of Mount Everest, which is nearly 5.5 miles (9 kilometers) above sea level, the boiling point is only 160 °F (71 °C). This is because the higher you go, the lower the pressure of the air—so the water **molecules** can escape more easily into the air.

- Not all planets are made of rock. Saturn is nearly all gas. It is so light that it would float on water.

- The first person to understand what **volume** meant was Archimedes, a scientist in ancient Greece. When he got into his bath, he realized that his body made the level of the water rise. The amount of water pushed up was exactly the same as the amount of space his body took up—his volume.

- The largest hailstone ever recorded was found in Kansas. It was an amazing 7.5 inches (19 centimeters) across and weighed almost 2 pounds (758 g)!

- Snowflakes are tiny **crystals** of ice. Each one has six arms. No two snowflakes are ever identical.

Glossary

appearance what something or someone looks like

atom one of the tiny particles of which matter is made

bleach chemical used to remove unwanted color or stains

change of state change from one state of matter to another

chemical change change in which something new is made

condense cool a gas so that it turns into a liquid

crystal hard substance with molecules that are arranged in a regular pattern

dissolve dissapear in a way. Sugar dissolves in water.

evaporate change from liquid to a gas

force a push or a pull that moves an object or changes its direction

freeze cool a liquid so that it turns into a solid

irreversible change that can only go one way

machine anything made to help human beings do some task, such as a car, a computer, or an electric drill

material any substance you can use to make something else

melt heat a solid so that it turns into a liquid

mixture result of mixing two or more materials together

mold container that holds a liquid to be set into a particular shape

molecule two or more atoms joined together

physical change change from one state of matter to another

plaster of Paris fine white powder that can be mixed with water to make models

precipitation water that falls to the earth as rain, snow, or hail

randomly something that happens in a disorganized, uncontrolled way

reversible change that can go backward or forward

solution liquid that has particles of a solid in it that can no longer be seen separate from the liquid

state of matter a solid, a liquid, or a gas

suspension liquid that has particles of a solid in it that can still be seen as separate particles

vapor liquid in its gas state

volume amount of space that something takes up

Index

More Books to Read

Glover, David. *Solids and Liquids: Science Facts and Experiments.*
    New York: Larousse Kingfisher Chambers, Inc., 2002.

Oxlade, Chris. *Chemicals in Action: Solids, Liquids and Gases.*
    Chicago: Heinemann Library, 2002.

Snedden, Robert. *Material World: Solids, Liquids & Gases.*
    Chicago: Heinemann Library, 2002.